Who's Your Idol?™

TAYLOR HICKS

Sally Ganchy

rosen publishing's
rosen central

New York

To Bippy

Published in 2008 by The Rosen Publishing Group, Inc.
29 East 21st Street, New York, NY 10010

Library of Congress Cataloging-in-Publication Data

Ganchy, Sally.
Taylor Hicks / Sally Ganchy. — 1st ed.
    p.cm. — (Who's your idol?)
Includes bibliographical references (p. 45) and index.
ISBN-13: 978-1-4042-1368-5 (library binding)
1. Hicks, Taylor, 1976—Juvenile literature. 2. Singers–United
States–Biography—Juvenile literature. I. Title.
ML3930.H455G36 2008
782.42164092—dc22
(B)
2007040995

Manufactured in the United States of America

Contents

Introduction

Taylor Hicks wasn't born a star. He wasn't rich, didn't look like a model, and wasn't born into a musical family. However, Hicks had a passion for soul music and a burning desire to share that music with others.

As a teenager, he taught himself to play the guitar and harmonica, and he developed a unique singing style. Hicks learned how to write songs, manage a band, and promote his music. No matter how many disappointments he faced and no matter how many obstacles he encountered, Hicks never gave up. When he finally got his chance at stardom on the hit television program *American Idol*, he was ready to seize the spotlight.

Few people believed Taylor Hicks would ever become a star. Sometimes, he didn't believe it himself. His story proves that with hard work and ambition, anything is possible.

Chapter 1

UNLIKELY BEGINNINGS

Taylor Reuben Hicks was born on October 7, 1976, in Birmingham, Alabama. His father, Bradley, was a dentist. His mother, Pamela, was an outgoing, carefree woman—the opposite of his quiet, responsible dad. Their differences led them to separate when Taylor was just four years old.

He went to live with his mother. Pamela never stayed at one apartment or job for long, so Taylor and his mom were constantly on the move. These early years were difficult for him. His mother loved him very much, but she had a drinking problem, and it wasn't easy for her to take care of herself and her child.

Eventually, Taylor's father went to court to win custody of him. In his autobiography, *Heart Full of Soul*, Hicks wrote, "The judge asked me in a thick Alabama accent, 'So, son, does your mother drink?' What could I say? For the record, here's

Growing up, Hicks enjoyed playing basketball, soccer, and baseball. Above, Hicks is pictured in his Simmons Middle School Tigers basketball uniform in 1990.

what I did say: 'Yes, sir, she sure does.'" The whole courtroom dissolved into laughter. Like many children of broken homes, Taylor learned early how to make the people around him smile.

The Lost Boy

At age eight, Taylor moved to suburban Hoover, Alabama, to live with his father. He would also be living with his father's new family: stepmother, Linda; younger stepbrother, Jeremy; and half-brother, Sean. He was thrilled to be living with a "whole" family, but he sometimes felt like it wasn't quite *his* family. His father was very different from his mother—he believed in discipline and responsibility, and he could be hard on Taylor.

Sometimes uncomfortable in his own home, young Taylor spent lots of time with his paternal grandparents, Jonie and Earl. He also loved to visit his friends' houses. On one of these visits, he made a discovery that changed his entire life.

Sweet Soul Music

Taylor loved listening to music. He often sang along to the car radio. But he didn't have a favorite type of music. Then, one day in fourth grade, he happened to listen to an old record called *The Best of Otis Redding* at his friend Greg Garnette's house. He was transfixed by Redding's music. When Greg wasn't looking, Taylor put the album in his book bag. Back home, he listened to it constantly.

Soul music became an obsession for Taylor. He was soon discovering musical legends like Aretha Franklin, Sam Cooke, Joe Cocker, and Marvin Gaye. One musician in particular, Ray Charles, became his hero. He found that he connected with the stories of pain, loss, suffering, joy, and deep emotion he heard on these artists' soul records. Taylor had found his music.

Going Gray

Taylor had always felt different because of his broken family. At the age of thirteen, something happened that made him really stand out from the crowd. He had been born with blond hair, but his hair had turned dark brown as he got older. Now, his first gray hairs started appearing. Other kids teased Taylor, and he became upset and embarrassed. By the time he was twenty, all of his hair had gone gray. Eventually, he was able to embrace this difference and celebrate it. Gray hair would become his trademark.

Ray Charles

Ray Charles (1930–2004) was a legendary performer and songwriter who revolutionized American music. A blind piano virtuoso with a husky voice, Charles combined the music genres of gospel, rhythm and blues, soul, and country to forge a unique sound. Many have described his first hit song, "I Got a Woman," as the first soul recording. Hits like

Ray Charles performs at a jazz festival in France in 2000. Hicks once likened soul music to a tree, with all kinds of branches. At the base of the tree, he said, is Ray Charles.

"I Can't Stop Loving You," "Hit the Road Jack," and his version of Hoagy Carmichael's "Georgia on My Mind" (now Georgia's official state song) remain popular. He even became the subject of a hit movie, *Ray*, starring Jamie Foxx. Charles has influenced generation after generation of musicians. When Taylor Hicks became a musician himself, he carried a small statue of Charles with him whenever he performed. Because his hair was gray and he sounded like Charles, fans gave Hicks the nickname "Gray Charles."

Becoming a Musician

In high school, Taylor was a popular kid with friends from many different groups. He played varsity basketball, soccer, and baseball. But his true love was music. At sixteen, he bought a harmonica for $2 at a flea market. He quickly became obsessed with the instrument, teaching himself to play along with his favorite records.

A teacher at school showed him how to play a couple of chords on the guitar as well. Richard Black, the father of one of his closest friends, also helped him develop his musical skills. Black was an amateur musician who had a complete sound studio in his garage. Taylor spent hours playing with the many different instruments. Black encouraged him to start writing his own songs. In addition, he taught Taylor that it wasn't enough to play and sing: in order to be successful, musicians must also be entertainers.

Taylor's enthusiasm paid off when he won first prize singing "Sweet Home Alabama" in his school talent competition. It gave him a taste of victory that he would experience many years later in another musical contest: *American Idol.*

Club Musician

Taylor was soon sitting in with local bands. Once his father even caught him playing in a bar. Taylor told *People* magazine, "I was playing one night, and my folks came for dinner. They came

Hicks, playing harmonica, performs with a music teacher at Berry High School in 1994. Hicks's victory in a high school talent show was an important self-esteem booster.

up to me and said, 'What . . . are you doing here?' My dad said, 'Son, you know that you're a minor and I'm your father,' and I was like, 'Dad, don't sweat it. It's just the blues.'" It was one of many struggles between a young man in love with music and a father trying to make sure his son did the right thing.

College Bands

Hicks wasn't a great student, but his father insisted he go to college. In 1995, he enrolled in Alabama's Auburn University. During his time there, Hicks studied journalism, psychology, business, and marketing. But his real education was outside the classroom, playing music at local clubs and bars. His schoolwork suffered, but his musical life thrived. He played with a jam band called Passing Through and an eclectic musical group called Fletch Lives. With these groups, Hicks toured Alabama, Florida, and Mississippi. He played in bars, in small clubs, and at fraternity parties. His confidence grew with each experience. He learned to entertain and connect with many different types of audiences.

His confidence as a musical group leader and songwriter was also growing. He wanted to be recognized for his own music. Paying for it himself, Hicks recorded his very first CD, *In Your Time*, and pressed 1,500 copies. Unfortunately, he found it was easier to make a CD than to sell it. His frustration only convinced him that he needed to work harder.

Nashville Dreams

By now, Hicks was a senior in college. He needed only thirty more credits to graduate. However, he was too impatient to earn a college degree that he felt he might never need. Instead of finishing college, he moved to Nashville, Tennessee, the epicenter of the U.S. country music industry. He was confident he'd be discovered there and become a huge star.

His time in Nashville was a bitter disappointment. He was unable to get a gig, get a record deal, or sell songs to other artists. Finally, after a year of struggle, Hicks realized he would never be a cookie-cutter country music star. In his autobiography, he said, "It struck me that if I was going to make it, I was going to have to do it not by fitting in but by standing out."

Working Musician

Hicks left Nashville and returned home to Alabama, where he put together the Taylor Hicks Band. His new plan was to get attention and win fans on the road, traveling wherever he could find an audience. It wasn't easy. He had to book his own gigs, put up his own posters, do business with crooked club owners, and manage all the musicians in his band. It was hard work, but slowly the Taylor Hicks Band built up a following.

The band also learned to become real crowd-pleasers. They became the opening act at performances by established artists like James Brown, Jackson Browne, and Percy Sledge. Famous blues musician Kevin Moore, better known as Keb' Mo', would become a good friend.

Hicks performs with friend and collaborator Jon Cook in Birmingham, Alabama, in 2004. Hicks and Cook met at Auburn University in 1995, beginning a long collaboration. Cook was one of the musicians who traveled with Hicks to Los Angeles to meet music executives.

In Need of Change

Eventually, the stress of life on the road started to wear on Hicks. His father pressured him to give up his dreams of stardom and find a real job. For a short time, in 2004, he even gave up music to work in a nursing home. But Hicks wasn't cut out for anything but singing and playing music. Unwilling to return to the road, but unable to feel happy in a "real job," he played at weddings, bar mitzvahs, and parties closer to home.

He started work on a second album, again paying for the recording out of his own pocket. Unlike his first album, though, *Under the Radar* started to sell at local record stores.

Armed with the new CD, the Taylor Hicks Band traveled to Los Angeles, looking for a big break. They played at the House of Blues and at the Playboy Mansion. But Hicks found that the record industry insiders he met in Los Angeles agreed with the executives who had rejected him in Nashville. They didn't think they could sell his music. Again, he was disappointed. Now, he had to go back to square one. His music industry hopes and dreams seemed to be fading fast.

THE ROAD TO
AMERICAN IDOL

By 2005, Taylor Hicks knew he needed a big break or must give up on a big-time career. He decided to audition for *American Idol*. He turned twenty-eight just before auditions, and the following year he would be too old to enter. It was now or never.

American Idol

American Idol is a reality TV contest for America's undiscovered young singers. Thousands audition each year. Judges select the best twenty-four singers to compete—and then the nation votes. Each week, singers with the least votes are eliminated. At the end of the season, the singer with the most votes wins a major-label recording contract and instant stardom. Since its debut in 2002, *American Idol* has launched the careers of Kelly Clarkson, Ruben Studdard, Clay Aiken, Fantasia Barrino, Jennifer Hudson, Bo Bice, and Carrie Underwood.

With his gray hair and husky voice, Taylor Hicks was an unlikely candidate for pop stardom. Even if he had looked and sounded the part, the chances he would succeed were one in a million. In fact, according to his autobiography, when his father learned he was auditioning for *American Idol*, he asked, "Why don't you just buy a lottery ticket?"

Besides acting as the host of *American Idol*, Ryan Seacrest is also a popular national radio DJ and an entrepreneur. Seacrest introduced Hicks's first live *American Idol* performance by saying, "He's got Joe Cocker's voice and Jay Leno's hair."

The Road to *Idol*

In August 2005, just before the *American Idol* auditions, Hicks visited New Orleans, Louisiana, to attend the wedding of his friends Brian and Tracy Grubb. The weekend of the wedding, Hurricane Katrina headed straight for New Orleans.

At the time, no one was certain that Hurricane Katrina would actually hit the city. At the reception, many guests announced they did not want to evacuate. Hicks, however, sensed impending disaster. At 3:00 AM the next morning, he decided to flee the city. He was just ahead of the storm. He offered a cab driver $500 to take him to the airport. Not the New Orleans Airport—all flights had been canceled there. Instead, he took the cab to West Monroe, Louisiana. Hicks bought a new ticket and flew home to Alabama. After the storm, he, along with the rest of the country, watched the devastating effects of Hurricane Katrina unfold on television.

There were so many hurricane refugees in all southern cities that *American Idol*'s auditions in Memphis, Tennessee, were canceled. But Hicks had an ace in the hole. As compensation for his canceled flight from New Orleans, Southwest Airlines had

Hurricane Katrina

Hurricane Katrina devastated the U.S. Gulf Coast. One of the hardest-hit cities was New Orleans, Louisiana, the birthplace of jazz. New Orleans is below sea level, protected from the waters of the mighty Mississippi River by a network of levees. Shortly after the hurricane, it became clear that some levees had failed, allowing the river to flood parts of the city. Due to the slow response of the Federal Emergency Management Agency (FEMA), many city residents became trapped in the deluge and perished. When the waters finally receded, large sections of New Orleans had been utterly destroyed. Hurricane Katrina became one of the worst natural disasters in U.S. history.

given him a free flight to anywhere in the country. So, he flew to Las Vegas, Nevada, for the *American Idol* auditions there.

The Las Vegas Auditions

At the auditions, Hicks was given the number 74,094. He was surrounded by thousands of hopeful singers, many of them younger and more fashionable than him. No one looking for America's next pop sensation would have picked Hicks. But he had already decided to stop trying to be a typical pop star. He was determined to just be himself.

The Judges

Over several TV seasons, the *Idol* judges have become household names. Randy Jackson, who has performed as a bassist with countless stars, always knows whether a contestant has slipped off-key.

Above, Hicks auditions for *American Idol* in Las Vegas in November 2005. His soulful, husky voice and down-home charm wowed Paula Abdul and Randy Jackson but left Simon Cowell cold.

Choreographer and pop star Paula Abdul is compassionate and gentle. Simon Cowell, the caustic British music-industry insider, says exactly what he thinks—and is often outrageously rude.

Now, Taylor Hicks stood before them. "Why are you here?" demanded Cowell. "Because I want my voice to be heard," Hicks replied in his slight southern drawl. "Why?" Cowell shot back. "Because I feel like I've got one," he said and then launched into Sam Cooke's classic song of hope and protest, "A Change Is Gonna Come." His voice was raspy, soft, and

Judges Simon Cowell, Paula Abdul, and Randy Jackson have gained fame and recognition in their *American Idol* roles. Here, they show their appreciation to *American Idol*'s fans.

sincere—definitely different. Hicks put his heart and soul into his fifteen seconds. Abdul exclaimed, "I did not expect that. You definitely can sing." He followed up with Ray Charles's upbeat "Swanee River Rock." He relaxed into a boyish grin and started to clap, stomp, and move. Jackson lit up, saying Hicks reminded him of Charles and Joe Cocker.

But Cowell stated frankly, "My problem is, it's not all about the voice, and you prove that." He said Hicks had no charisma; he should sing backup vocals. Abdul and Jackson disagreed: How could someone with Hicks's distinctive moves sing backup? And how could they know whether he had star quality unless they gave him a chance?

Cowell gave Hicks a definitive no, saying the other two judges "will not put you in the group to be judged by the public." But Hicks needed only two votes to proceed to the next round, and Jackson and Abdul both said yes. "You're going to Hollywood!" Abdul shouted. Hicks whooped. As he walked out of the audition room, Jackson said excitedly, "Bring all the Cocker, all the Ray Charles . . . come on, man!"

Hollywood Week

Hicks finally had a real shot at stardom. But now he had to survive Hollywood Week, the next round of eliminations. In Hollywood, Taylor met some of the country's most promising young talents. There were handsome contestants, like Ace Young. There were charming contestants such as Kellie Pickler, whose sincerity won everyone over. There were great artists, like soulful Paris

Bennett. There were singers with big personalities such as catty Brenna Gethers. And there were contestants who had it all— like Katharine McPhee, the daughter of a vocal coach, whose effortless beauty was matched by her incredible voice.

Choosing his songs wisely, Hicks made it through the first rounds of cuts. When it came time to choose the top twenty-four contestants, each remaining singer was told separately whether or not he or she made the cut. Everyone had to walk the length of a long room to the table where the judges sat. Hicks decided to make a real impression. He played the harmonica and grooved his way the whole length of the room. Jackson exclaimed, "What an entrance!" Abdul reminded Hicks that Cowell predicted he'd never make it to the finals. His face fell . . . until she said, "Congratulations, my dear, you're through."

The Top Twenty-Four

Hicks had made it past the judges. Now, he had to connect with the television audience the way he'd connected with crowds throughout the Southeast.

Twelve males were competing for six male slots, and Hicks was up against some great singers. Rocker Chris Daughtry's powerful voice never faltered. Elliott Yamin's first live performance inspired Cowell to say that he had the potential to be the best male vocalist to ever appear on *American Idol*.

For his first song, Hicks selected "Levon," made famous by Elton John. He started out simply and seriously but soon blasted out the refrain. Some of the other contestants had been nervous, stilted, and a little plastic. But Hicks's love for music shone through every note—he was clearly absorbed in his performance. Jackson told him, "There's never been anyone on this show in five years like you." But Hicks's greatest praise of the night came from Cowell, who told him, "I said in the beginning, if you remember, that I didn't think you should make the finals of this competition. I was wrong."

Soul Patrol!

Hicks was ecstatic. He told the show's host, Ryan Seacrest, "If music's in your heart, you feel it, you play it, you sing it, you perform it, you bust your buns doing it." And then he looked straight into the camera and shouted "Soul Patrol! Do it, baby! Soul Patrol!"

Seacrest was bewildered, but fans at home were ecstatic. Hicks's fans had voted online to call themselves the "Soul Patrol." They loved the fact that he was reaching out directly to them on national television. Over time, the Soul Patrol became a close and overwhelmingly dedicated group of fans.

To the Top Twelve

Hicks tried constantly to surprise the public. Sometimes it worked, and sometimes it didn't. His rendition of the Commodores' "Easy" left the judges feeling as if he hadn't tried hard enough. His performance of the Doobie Brothers' "Taking It to the Streets,"

One of the Soul Patrol waves a sign in the audience of an
American Idol show in 2006. On the March 28, 2006, show, Hicks
explained to host Ryan Seacrest, "[The] Soul Patrol is a legion of fans that
were with me right from the very beginning, when I was a gray-headed guy
in Las Vegas, and they stuck with me, through thick and thin."

however, was a hit. For the first time, Hicks danced maniacally
across the stage. Abdul gave him a standing ovation. "I'll be
using those steps for the rest of my life!" the petite choreographer
gushed. Cowell simply raised his eyebrows and said, "Taylor,
you single-handedly could kill the music-video industry."

But what Cowell thought didn't matter so much anymore.
Hicks had made it to the Top Twelve.

Chapter 3

THE AMERICAN IDOL

Taylor Hicks was used to performing for hours every week. For *American Idol*, he had to squeeze all of that music into just a few moments on-screen. He was also incredibly busy. He had to choose songs, rehearse with the *American Idol* band, and learn group musical numbers. He also discovered that the life of a celebrity musician isn't all about music: he gave interviews, participated in photo shoots, and filmed commercials.

Now, Hicks and the other Top-Twelve contestants moved from their hotel into *American Idol* dorms, where he shared a room with Elliott Yamin. He and Yamin would become close friends. The show's venue had changed, too. The Top Twelve were competing in a bigger theater, with a huge audience and band. But, most important, each *American Idol* week would now have a theme and a special guest to help contestants shine. Hicks got to meet and work with famous artists like Stevie Wonder, Barry Manilow, Kenny Rogers, Andrea Bocelli, the rock band Queen, and Rod Stewart!

Performances of a Lifetime

Over the course of the show, Hicks had plenty of ups and downs. During Stevie Wonder's week, Hicks blew away the audience and judges with his heartfelt, passionate rendition of "Living for the City." But not all of his performances were hits. "Country Week" was particularly rough for him. He chose to sing "Take Me Home, Country Roads," which his friend Keb' Mo' had warned him not to sing. Even guest Kenny Rogers recognized that Hicks was having trouble connecting with the song. The judges called his performance lackluster.

Luckily, the next week Hicks sang Queen's "Crazy Little Thing Called Love." He danced up and down the stage stairs, jumped in the air, and even kicked over the microphone stand! Paula Abdul, who loved his performance, marveled, "I don't know whether we should give you a record deal or a straitjacket!" Simon Cowell, however, was not impressed. Luckily, fans thought it was one of Hicks's best performances.

During "Great American Song Book Week," he got to meet one of his heroes, Rod Stewart. Stewart loved Hicks. In fact, he defended Hicks against Cowell's recent attacks: "Simon said about Taylor that this is not a dance competition; this is a singing competition. Well, I disagree. I think you must do everything that you possibly can within reason to sell the song. And I think he's

Taylor Hicks and the other Season Five finalists pose with members of the legendary rock band Queen. Hicks is in the back row, to the right of fellow finalists Bucky Covington *(center)* and Chris Daughtry *(left)*. In the front row are Elliott Yamin *(far right)* and Katharine McPhee *(far left)*.

a pretty good mover!" Hicks's "Great American Song" was Sam Cooke's "You Send Me." His simple yet sophisticated performance was one of his greatest *American Idol* moments.

Rising to the Top

Sometimes, Hicks's performances could be divisive. His rendition of Wild Cherry's "Play that Funky Music" was almost out of control. He danced into the audience, worked up a sweat, and

The Rebel

In front of *American Idol's* cameras, Taylor Hicks always stuck out. He was a rebel behind the scenes, too. When he was chosen as one of the Top Twenty-Four, Hicks was asked to sign a contract with the show's producers. He felt that the contract wasn't fair and tried to convince his fellow contestants to refuse to sign. His attempt to organize the Idols didn't work, and luckily, he signed the contract anyway. Later on, Hicks rebelled in smaller ways, such as getting fellow contestants Elliott Yamin and Bucky Covington to violate their producers' orders and sneak out for a night on the town in Las Vegas. Even his song choices sometimes sparked controversy. For "Classic Love Songs Week," the contestants met with famous blind opera singer Andrea Bocelli and composer-producer David Foster. Hicks wanted to sing Otis Redding's "Try a Little Tenderness," but the show's producers forced him to change his song at the last minute. He sang "Just Once" by James Ingram instead.

at the end of the song collapsed onto the ground. Paula Abdul loved the performance, Simon Cowell hated it, and Randy Jackson was unsure. Host Ryan Seacrest, in a show of solidarity, fell down on the floor next to Hicks after the judges' comments.

But that very same show, he gave a performance on which everyone could agree. He sang "Something" by the Beatles'

George Harrison. The performance was the exact opposite of his first song of the night: vulnerable, heartfelt, and tender. It was a classic performance of a classic song. The judges—and the public—were enchanted.

Top Four

The field narrowed weekly, until there were just four contestants: songbird Katharine McPhee, rocker Chris Daughtry, joyful Elliott Yamin, and black sheep Taylor Hicks. By this point, each contestant had to sing two songs per show. The next week's theme was "Elvis Week."

In the taped introduction to the Elvis show, Hicks said, "When I heard that it was 'Elvis Week,' I thought to myself, 'Now I'm gonna have some fun.'" The contestants headed to Graceland, home of Elvis Presley, "the King" of rock n' roll. There they met Elvis's widow, Priscilla, and his daughter, Lisa Marie. They even got to drive around the estate on one of Elvis's famous golf carts.

Hicks put on a fun show for his first Elvis song, "Jailhouse Rock." But his true breakthrough came on the classic ballad "In the Ghetto." That week's guest, music mogul Tommy Mottola, had advised him to keep his performance simple and sincere. Hicks did just that, delivering one of his most heartfelt performances. Jackson summed it all up by saying, "The right key for you, finally. The right song for you, finally. When and if you make a record, this is the kind of record you should make—that was hot, man!"

A smiling Cowell agreed: "You have just sung your way into the semifinals, young man!"

That week, more than any other time, it seemed uncertain who would make it through to the next round. To the surprise of many, Daughtry was voted off. Hicks, along with McPhee and Yamin, were now in the Final Three.

A Homecoming Fit for an Idol

Every season, *American Idol* flies the top three contestants back to their hometowns to greet their fans. Hicks was flown home to Birmingham, Alabama, on a private jet. After years of struggle and disappointment, he was suddenly the biggest star in town. He traveled the highway in a stretch SUV limo, with a police escort. He gave interviews on radio talk shows and at TV stations—he even participated in a local morning weather report!

Hicks was treated to a massive parade through the center of Birmingham. Thousands of cheering fans with homemade signs lined the street. Marching bands played, a beauty queen waved to the crowd, and cheerleaders marched shouting "We are the Soul Patrol!" Mayor Bernard Kinkaid even presented Hicks with the key to the city.

The next stop on the homecoming tour was Hoover, Alabama, where Hicks had attended high school. There, in one of Alabama's biggest malls, his old band played a concert for 12,000 fans. Next, he met Alabama governor Bob Riley. The

Hicks waves to adoring fans at his homecoming parade in Birmingham, Alabama, on May 12, 2006. It was a day of support and celebration beyond his wildest dreams.

governor named May 12, 2006, "Taylor Hicks Day in Alabama." In return, Hicks made the governor and his wife official members of the Soul Patrol. It was more than a dream come true—it was beyond Hicks's wildest dreams.

Top-Three Show

The next week on *American Idol*, Hicks had to perform three songs. First was Bruce Springsteen's "Dancing in the Dark," chosen for him by his future boss, record producer Clive Davis. During the performance, Hicks pulled Abdul onstage to dance with him! Jackson chose Hicks's next song, Joe Cocker's classic ballad "You Are So Beautiful." Hicks's interpretation was raw, even pained, with an incredible falsetto run in the middle of the song. Cowell told him, "Taylor, for me, that was far and away your best performance so far." The last song was Hicks's own choice—the very first soul song he ever fell in love with, Otis Redding's "Try a Little Tenderness." After his energetic, intense performances that night, Hicks seemed unstoppable.

The voting for the Top Two was incredibly close. By a hair, the finalists were Taylor Hicks and Katherine McPhee. McPhee might have had an incredible voice and model-perfect looks, but Hicks had experience, heart, and soul. It would be a fight to the finish—and America would decide the winner.

The Finals

The final competition took place at Los Angeles's Kodak Theatre. In the audience were the other Top Twenty-Four contestants, as well as celebrities like Mandy Moore, Ben Stiller, and Tori Spelling. Hick's father, Bradley; his stepmother, Linda; and his brothers sat near the front of the theater. They looked proud, nervous, and happy. Their boy had finally made it to the big time.

The pressure was really on now. Host Ryan Seacrest asked the judges to give the contestants some advice. Cowell wryly offered, "I would suggest that the contestants pray that the other one forget the words."

The night's first two songs from each contestant were favorites from earlier shows in the competition. Hicks's first selection, "Living for the City," suited him perfectly. Wearing a purple jacket in order to stand out, he showed his originality by throwing his entire self into the performance and dancing through the audience. The crowd went absolutely wild. Even Cowell was pleased, saying, "It was a great way to start the show. It's arguably the worst jacket I've ever seen in my life, but what do I know?"

Hicks performs "Living for the City" during the *American Idol* finals on May 23, 2006, at the Kodak Theatre in Hollywood, California. Hicks found the distinctive purple velvet jacket, which Simon Cowell hated, in a thrift store.

His passionate performance had blown Katharine McPhee's out of the water. But McPhee brought the house down with her stunning version of "Somewhere Over the Rainbow." Hicks's reprise of "Levon" paled by comparison. Cowell announced that McPhee had taken the second round.

McPhee and Hicks then premiered their first singles. These singles would be their first commercial releases, no matter who won the competition. McPhee sang "My Destiny" well, but Hicks had saved the best for last. His new single, "Do I Make You Proud?" started slow and soft, and then built to a crescendo. At the song's climax, a gospel choir joined in. Hicks couldn't keep the grin off his face as he sang the words that fit the occasion so well: "Stronger than I've ever been/Never been afraid of standing out/Do I make you proud?" Afterward, Cowell said solemnly, "Assuming that I was right that the show was tied, then you've just won *American Idol*." Abdul and Jackson turned with huge smiles to Cowell, saying "I told you so!" They wouldn't let him forget that he had originally not wanted to put Hicks on the show.

The Finale

American Idol's Season Five finale was the television event of the season. There were many special musical guests: Mary J. Blige, Prince, Burt Bacharach, Dionne Warwick, Al Jarreau, Meat Loaf, and previous *American Idol* winner Carrie Underwood. Hicks performed a duet of Elvis's "In the Ghetto" with R & B singer Toni Braxton. Then came the moment everyone was waiting for. As the audience held their breath, Seacrest announced that the newest American Idol was . . . Taylor Hicks!

Hicks celebrates onstage after winning Season Five of *American Idol*. Hicks's victory surprised many people who saw him as the contest's underdog.

Hicks later wrote in his autobiography, "As I walked onto the Kodak stage that night with a heart full of soul and took my place in the spotlight, it wasn't nerves I was feeling, but something else entirely. In truth, I felt right at home—a man in the right place at the right time. What was once a bubble had somehow become home—and really, home was what I'd been looking for all along."

And so Hicks took the stage to perform his new single, "Do I Make You Proud?" It was an emotional moment for everyone. As the song reached its climax, he shouted out, "Come on, America! I'm living the American Dream!" Fireworks exploded, confetti fell, and the gospel choir sang. Against all the odds, Taylor Hicks had triumphed.

AFTER *IDOL*

Taylor Hicks became an instant star. As the newest American Idol, he gave interviews, made public appearances, and starred in commercials. His single "Do I Make You Proud?" debuted at number 1 on the *Billboard* magazine charts. He was sent screenplays for films that he could star in. His independent album, *In Your Time*, which he had once given away, started selling for $100 on the Internet auction site eBay. He was parodied on *Saturday Night Live* and named *People* magazine's Hottest Bachelor of 2006. Hicks even signed a deal with an imprint of the book publisher Random House to write an inspirational autobiography.

From Ray to Gray

Hicks had been overjoyed to introduce a generation of young Americans to

Taylor Hicks performs in New York City's Bryant Park on July 21, 2006, as a part of *Good Morning America*'s summer concert series. Hicks loves touring the country with his band.

soul music greats such as Sam Cooke, Joe Cocker, and Ray Charles. Now, that mission earned him an opportunity beyond his wildest dreams.

He received a personal tour of his idol Ray Charles's home recording studio. The studio and house had been untouched since Charles had passed away. Hicks wandered through the vaults of rare tapes—a virtual gold mine to a dedicated fan like him. The Ray Charles Marketing Group offered Hicks the opportunity to record his next album in Charles's studio—making him the first outside artist ever to receive such an invitation. He even got a chance to try on one of Charles's jackets and was shocked to find that it fit!

American Idol Live

Before Hicks could record anything, he had to star in the "Pop-Tarts Presents *American Idol* Live" tour with his fellow finalists. It was a great opportunity for him: he got to work with great musicians, reach out to thousands of fans, and introduce America to soul classics. On the tour, he discovered that he didn't love singing in arenas. He still preferred smaller clubs, where he could play as much as he liked and make a personal connection with people in the audience.

Luckily, he had arranged a way to play some small clubs in many "*American Idol* Live" tour cities. His old band had been playing without him as the Little Memphis Blues Orchestra. Now, they toured to many of the same cities, on the same nights, as the *Idol* tour. Hicks got rushed from his set at the tour to sit in with his friends late at night. This gave him a chance to cut loose a little, play harmonica and guitar, and reconnect with audiences in closer quarters.

Idols in the White House

Hicks's unfailing talent for self-promotion led to one very unexpected place: the White House. His ninth-grade English

Hicks and his fellow top-nine *American Idol* contestants visit the president in the White House on July 28, 2006. In the center of the back row, Taylor Hicks and Katharine McPhee stand next to President Bush.

teacher had gotten a job as First Lady Laura Bush's press secretary. Hicks had been in touch with his former teacher periodically throughout his time on *American Idol*, and she was rooting for him on Capitol Hill. Now that the *Idol* tour was due to swing through Washington, D.C., Hicks asked her if the Idols could meet the president of the United States. To his surprise, she said yes. He and the other Idols met with George W. Bush in the Oval Office for a short time and got their pictures taken with him. It was a truly incredible opportunity for all of the performers.

Taylor Hicks Records *Taylor Hicks*

After the "*American Idol* Live" tour ended in fall 2006, it was time for Hicks to record his first major-label release. He later wrote, "This was the fulfillment of all my dreams—much more than just winning a competition, even a very big one, on TV. For me, making that album was like finally getting my shot to play major-league ball, as opposed to just the ego stroke of going high in the draft."

The schedule was tight, since the record company hoped to record and produce the album in time for Christmas. Hicks and his producer, Matt Serletic, managed to put together an album. The new release, titled *Taylor Hicks*, mixed some of the *Idol* winner's original songs ("Soul Thing" and "The Deal") with covers and songs written just for him by great songwriters like Bryan Adams ("The Right Place") and Rob Thomas of Matchbox 20 ("Dream Myself Awake"). Hicks's debut album went platinum, reaching number 2 on the Billboard charts.

On the Road Again

However, many industry insiders predicted that Hicks would not sell as many records as *American Idol* winners from past seasons. Although the country had chosen him, Hicks seemed too far outside the mainstream of American pop music to do well. Radio stations didn't know how to classify his throwback sound, and sales couldn't be strong without radio support.

Still, releasing the album was a dream come true for Hicks. During the next year, he got to sit in with musical heroes Willie Nelson, Widespread Panic, and the Allman Brothers Band. He sang a duet with the great singer Gladys Knight during the Orange Bowl's halftime show. He also sang Christmas carols for the lighting ceremony of the giant Christmas tree at Rockefeller Center in New York City.

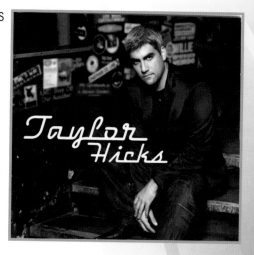

Just a few months after winning *American Idol*, Hicks recorded his major-label debut, *Taylor Hicks*. The album was released on December 12, 2006.

In many interviews, Hicks has stated that his dream is to tour forever, playing mid-sized clubs and theaters with a great band and his own tour bus, building a dedicated fan base that will follow his career. Before winning *American Idol*, he told *USA Today*, "My home has been the road, even before *American Idol* . . . A tour bus with some good cold iceberg lettuce, that's where I'll stay." In 2007, he took his first real tour of the United States.

Taylor Hicks went from a zero to a hero on *American Idol*, and now he is playing for keeps. He dreamed his whole life of being a successful musician. And now, no matter what the future may bring, that dream is a reality.

Glossary

amateur Someone who takes part in something for pleasure rather than for pay.

autobiography A book telling the story of the writer's life.

Billboard charts Charts that rank the number of sales for the most popular musical recordings in a variety of categories.

blues African American folk music characterized by lyrical repetition, a twelve-bar structure, and the expression of emotions like rage, sorrow, and loss.

catty Mean or spiteful.

caustic Sarcastic in a bitter or other way that causes bad feelings.

charisma The ability to attract or influence others.

choreographer A person who composes dances. Choreographers can work in a wide variety of dance styles, from ballet to cheerleading routines to music videos.

crescendo A gradual increase in the volume of a piece of music.

deluge A great flood.

epicenter Literally, the point on the earth's surface directly above the origin of an earthquake. In metaphor, a center of power or action.

evacuate To escape a location that is, or could become, unsafe.

falsetto A method used by male singers to sing in a very high voice.

gig Slang term for a music job; a scheduled musical performance.

gospel A rousing genre of music that originated in the African American church.

jazz An American musical genre forged from blues and ragtime. Group and solo improvisation play an important role in jazz.

key A tonal center around which a piece of music is organized. Pop singers must find a good key for each song that they sing in order to showcase their vocal range.

lackluster Lacking sparkle or shine; disappointing; dull.

levee A man-made embankment designed to keep a river from flooding the surrounding areas.

parodied Written or performed imitation that deliberately copies another work in a comic way.

paternal Related to one's father or being on the father's side of the family.

rhythm and blues (R & B) A musical genre that originated from African American communities in the 1940s. The term once meant a combination of blues and jazz that became a forerunner of rock 'n' roll. Today, R & B is soulful pop music that often incorporates elements of hip-hop and funk.

soul music A musical genre that fuses gospel music, blues, and R & B.

stilted Lacking fluency; being halting in flow.

transfixed Shocked into silence and unable to move.

virtuoso A musician with exceptional technique and ability.

vulnerable Sensitive, or easily hurt or damaged.

For More Information

The Blues Foundation
49 Union Avenue
Memphis, TN 38103-2492
(901) 527-2583
Web site: http://www.blues.org
  This nonprofit organization's goal is to preserve blues history, celebrate
  blues excellence, support blues education, and ensure the future of this
  American art form.

Fox Broadcasting Company
P.O. Box 900
Beverly Hills, CA 902130900
Web site: http://www.fox.com
  Fox's Web site has information on the network's shows, including
  American Idol.

New Orleans Jazz & Heritage Festival and Foundation, Inc.
1205 North Rampart Street
New Orleans, LA 70116
(504) 558-6100
Web site: http://www.jazzandheritage.org
  This nonprofit organization works to preserve the music, arts, culture, and
  heritage of Louisiana jazz through its annual Jazz Fest and other festivals
  and programs.

Ray Charles Enterprises
2107 West Washington Boulevard, Suite 200
Los Angeles, CA 90018
(323) 737-8000
Web site: http://www.raycharles.com
   The Ray Charles Enterprises Web site offers a wealth of information about
   the legendary singer.

Stax Museum of American Soul Music
926 East McLemore Avenue
Memphis, TN 38106
(901) 946-2535
Web site: http://www.soulsvilleusa.com
   This museum pays tribute to the soul music artists that recorded at the
   original site of Stax Records. Al Green, Otis Redding, and other soul
   pioneers are showcased.

Web Sites

Due to the changing nature of Internet links, Rosen Publishing
has developed an online list of Web sites related to the subject
of this book. This site is updated regularly. Please use this link to
access the list:

http://www.rosenlinks.com/wyi/tahi

For Further Reading

Canfield, Jack, Mark Victor Hansen, and Debra Halperin Poneman. *Chicken Soup for the American Idol Soul: Featuring Stories from Top Idols from Every Season.* Deerfield Beach, FL: Health Communications, Inc., 2007.

Cowell, Simon. *I Don't Mean To Be Rude, But . . . Backstage Gossip from American Idol and the Secrets That Can Make You a Star.* New York, NY: Broadway Books, 2003.

Guralnick, Peter. *Sweet Soul Music: Rhythm and Blues and the Southern Dream of Freedom.* Boston, MA: Back Bay Books, 1999.

Hicks, Taylor. *Heart Full of Soul.* New York, NY: Crown Publishers, 2007.

Jackson, Randy, and K. C. Baker. *What's Up Dawg? How to Become a Superstar in the Music Business.* New York, NY: Hyperion, 2004.

Walsh, Marissa. *American Idol: The Search for a Superstar. The Official Book.* New York, NY: Bantam Books, 2002.

Bibliography

"All About Taylor Hicks." RealityTVMagazine.com. April 20, 2006. Retrieved August 2007 (http://www.realitytvmagazine.com/blog/2006/04/all_about_taylo.html).

"*American Idol* Contestants Get to Visit Real West Wing; Bush Squeezing in Reality Show's Winner, Finalists Between More Serious Business." *Houston Chronicle*, July 28, 2006.

Aquilante, Dan. "Never an Idle '*Idol*': Taylor Hicks Embraces Life of a Musical Gypsy." *New York Post*, December 10, 2006. Retrieved July 2007 (http://www.nypost.com/seven/12102006/entertainment/music/never_an_idle_idol_music_dan_aquilante.htm).

Carlson, Erin. "Taylor Hicks' Soul Patrol Seems to Be Losing Steam; The Transition from Reality TV Star to Established Singer Has Been Rough." *The Record*, March 4, 2007.

Dinh, Mai, and Janet Murphy, eds. "Taylor Hicks: Biography." People.com. Retrieved August 2007 (http://www.people.com/people/taylor_hicks/biography).

Graff, Gary. "Unlikely '*Idol*' Content with His Prospects." *Columbus Dispatch*, August 11, 2006. Retrieved August 15, 2007 (http://www.columbusdispatch.com/dispatch/contentbe/dispatch/2006/08/11/20060811-D1-03.html).

Greenblatt, Leah. "Taylor Made." EW.com, July 21, 2006. Retrieved August, 2007 (http://www.ew.com/ew/article/0,,1213673,00.html).

Hicks, Taylor, with David Wild. *Heart Full of Soul: An Inspirational Memoir About Finding Your Voice and Finding Your Way.* New York, NY: Crown Publishers, 2007.

Moss, Corey. "Taylor Hicks Excited About Chris Daughtry's Success, 'Obscure Covers.'" MTV.com. January 24, 2007. Retrieved August 2007 (http://www.mtv.com/news/articles/1550642/20070123/hicks_taylor.jhtml).

Moss, Corey. "Taylor Hicks Hopes 'Traveling Circus of Fans' Follows Him on Tour." MTV.com. December 11, 2006. Retrieved August 2007 (http://www.mtv.com/news/articles/1547600/20061208/hicks_taylor.jhtml).

Phares, Heather. "Taylor Hicks: Biography." AllMusic.com. Retrieved August 15, 2007 (http://www.allmusic.com/cg/amg.dll?p=amg&sql=11:3ifexqydld0e~T1).

Sculley, Alan. "Years of Work Pay Off for '*Idol*' Winner." *Virginian Pilot*, June 26, 2007.

Index

About the Author

Sally Ganchy is a music writer and teaching artist who loves old soul music. She has played fiddle in bluegrass, jazz, and hip-hop bands, and writes regularly for the Metropolitan Opera's Web site. She is an official member of the Soul Patrol.

Photo Credits

Cover (left) © Rob Loud/Getty Images; cover (middle, right), pp. 1, 35 © Bryan Bedder/Getty Images; p. 6 © Courtesy Simmons Middle School/Zuma Press; p. 8 © Vanina Lucchesi/AFP/Getty Images; p. 10 © Courtesy Berry High School/Zuma Press; p. 12 © Michael Sheehan/ www.furtherimages.com; pp. 15, 18 © Kevin Winter/Getty Images; p. 17 © Ray Mickshaw/WireImage/Getty Images; pp. 22, 31, 33 © Vince Bucci/Getty Images; p. 25 © Everett Collection; p. 29 © AP Images; p. 37 © Mark Wilson/Getty Images.

Designer: Tahara Anderson; **Photo Researcher:** Amy Feinberg